*"How Do You Think? The Journey Towards QA Excellence"
is a book that will explore the processes and mindset required
to achieve excellence in Software Quality Assurance (S-QA).
QA is a critical aspect of many industries, such as software
development, manufacturing, finance and healthcare, so it's
industry independent.*

"Dedicated to ALL who thrive for Digital QUALITY"

HOW DO YOU THINK?

SHREE NARAYAN JHA

INDIA • SINGAPORE • MALAYSIA

Preface

Welcome to "How Do You Think? The Journey Towards QA Excellence." In the world of Quality Assurance (QA), excellence is the pinnacle we all strive for. Whether you're a seasoned QA professional, a curious beginner, or a manager seeking to enhance your team's performance, this book is designed to be your guide on the path to achieving QA excellence.

But what exactly is QA excellence, and why is it important? We'll delve into these questions in the coming chapters, but let's begin with a simple thought experiment.

Imagine you're building a bridge—a vital connection that thousands of people will rely on every day. Would you want it to be strong, reliable, and free from any structural flaws? Of course, you would. Now, imagine you're developing a software application that controls life-saving medical equipment or a mobile app that manages people's financial transactions. Would you want these systems to be anything less than excellent in quality? Certainly not.

In today's fast-paced world, where technology evolves at breakneck speed and the demands for quality are higher than ever, excellence in QA is not an option; it's a necessity. It's the difference between a bridge that stands the test of time and one that crumbles, between software that works flawlessly and one that crashes when you need it the most.

So, how do we embark on this journey towards QA excellence? It starts with a question: "How do you think?" It's about the way we approach problems, analyse data, make decisions, and continuously improve. QA excellence isn't just about testing software or products; it's about thinking critically, creatively, and strategically.

In the pages that follow, we will explore the art and science of QA, the mindset and methodologies that lead to excellence, and the practical steps to elevate your QA processes. We'll learn from real-world examples, discover the latest tools and technologies, and uncover the secrets of those who have mastered the craft of QA.

Whether you're looking to enhance your QA team's performance, develop your own QA skills, or simply gain a deeper understanding of quality assurance in the modern world, this book is here to guide you on your journey. So, let's start on this adventure together, and let's find out: What do you think?

Contents

Chapter 7: The Human Element- QA Team Dynamics — 56

Chapter 8: Adapting to Agile and DevOps Environments — 63

Chapter 9: QA in the Era of AI and Machine Learning — 71

Chapter 1

The Quest for QA Excellence Begins

Introduction

In the world of Quality Assurance (QA), excellence isn't a destination; it's a journey. It's a journey that begins with a simple yet profound question: "How do you think?" This question lies at the heart of our quest for QA excellence. As we embark on this journey together, let's explore the foundational principles that underpin QA, examine the mindset required for success, and understand why QA is more important than ever in our rapidly evolving world.

The Essence of QA

Quality Assurance, often abbreviated as QA, is about ensuring that the products and processes we create meet or exceed the expectations of our users, customers, and stakeholders. It's the process of systematically checking, testing, and improving our work to eliminate defects, enhance performance, and deliver a superior experience.

Think about your favourite smartphone, the one that seamlessly connects you to the digital universe. Imagine the countless lines of code, intricate hardware components, and rigorous testing that go into crafting it. QA is what makes that phone a reliable companion, ensuring it doesn't freeze, crash, or compromise your data.

Or consider the pharmaceutical industry, where QA plays a life-or-death role. Before a new medication reaches your pharmacy, it undergoes rigorous testing to ensure it's safe and effective. QA is what stands between a life-altering breakthrough and a potential catastrophe.

In essence, QA is the guardian of quality, the gatekeeper of excellence. But achieving QA excellence isn't as simple as running tests or checking boxes on a checklist. It's a holistic approach that requires the right mindset, the right tools, and the right strategies.

The QA Mindset

At the core of QA excellence is a particular mindsets—an attitude and approach that embraces the pursuit of perfection and continuous improvement. It's a mindset that questions assumptions, seeks root causes, and never settles for mediocrity. This mindset is characterised by:

- **Curiosity:** QA professionals are inherently curious. They want to know why things work the way they do and why they sometimes fail. They're detectives, constantly seeking clues and answers.

- **Critical Thinking:** Critical thinking is the ability to objectively analyse information, identify flaws, and make informed decisions. In QA, critical thinking helps us spot defects and vulnerabilities that others might miss.

- **Attention to Detail:** The devil, as they say, is in the details. QA professionals have a keen eye for detail, spotting the smallest inconsistencies or irregularities that could impact quality.

- **Empathy:** QA isn't just about technical testing; it's also about understanding the end user's experience. Empathy helps us put ourselves in the shoes of our customers and ensure their needs are met.

- **Resilience:** QA professionals understand that failures and setbacks are part of the process. They don't get discouraged when defects are found; instead, they see each one as an opportunity for improvement.

Why QA Matters Today

In our fast-paced, interconnected world, the importance of QA has never been greater. Consider the following reasons why QA is essential in today's landscape:

- **Digital Transformation:** The shift to digital technologies has accelerated, and QA is at the forefront of ensuring that digital experiences are seamless, secure, and reliable.

- **Customer Expectations:** Consumers have higher expectations than ever before. They demand flawless experiences, and QA is the key to meeting those demands.

- **Data Protection:** With the increasing importance of data, security breaches can have catastrophic consequences. QA is vital in safeguarding sensitive information.

- **Continuous Improvement:** In an era of constant innovation, QA helps organisations adapt, evolve, and stay competitive.

Conclusion

As we journey through the chapters of this book, we'll explore how to cultivate the QA mindset, apply QA principles, and navigate the ever-evolving landscape of QA tools and technologies. Together, we'll uncover the path to QA excellence and equip you with the knowledge and skills to excel in the world of quality assurance.

So, are you ready to embark on this quest for QA excellence? It begins with "How do you think....?"

Pause. Introspect. Reflect.

Here are some **exercises** for Chapter 1, "The Quest for QA Excellence Begins", these questions are designed to encourage you to actively engage with the content of **Chapter 1** and apply the concepts based on your own experiences and understanding of quality assurance.

Exercise 1.1: Reflect on Your QA Journey

Question:

Reflect on your own experiences in quality assurance or a related field. What does quality assurance mean to you, and how have you approached it in your work or projects? Write a brief personal statement to capture your thoughts and experiences.

Exercise 1.2: QA Mindset Assessment

Questions:

On a scale of 1 to 5, where 1 represents "Not at all" and 5 represents "Completely," rate yourself on the following qualities:

- Curiosity

- Critical thinking

- Attention to detail

- Empathy

- Resilience

After completing the self-assessment, reflect on which area do your strengths lie in terms of the QA mindset, assess the areas you think could use improvement.

Exercise 1.3: Real-Life QA Examples

Questions:

- Share an example of a successful software release or project where QA played a critical role. Describe what aspects of the QA mindset contributed to this success.

- Think of a situation where QA failures resulted in a significant issue or setback. What elements of the QA mindset were missing or insufficient in this case, and how could they have made a difference?

Exercise 1.4: Exploring QA in Different Industries

Questions:

- Research and provide an example of how QA practices are applied in an industry other than software development, such as eCommerce, healthcare, manufacturing, or finance. Briefly summarise the example and explain how the QA mindset is crucial in that context.

- How do you think the principles of quality assurance discussed in this chapter can be adapted and applied to your own industry or field of expertise?

Exercise 1.5: QA in the Digital Age

Questions:

- Identify and list specific examples of how digital transformation has affected your life or your industry. How has this transformation impacted the quality of products or services?

- Consider the examples you listed in question 1. Explain how QA practices can help ensure the quality and reliability of digital experiences in these scenarios. What role does the QA mindset play in this process?

"Excellence is not being the best; it's doing your best—each and every time." — Shree

Chapter 2

The Fundamentals of Quality Assurance

Introduction

Now that we've laid the foundation for our journey towards QA excellence in Chapter 1, it's time to delve deeper into the fundamentals of Quality Assurance (QA). In this chapter, we'll explore the key principles, methodologies, and practices that underpin the world of QA. By understanding these fundamentals, you'll be better equipped to navigate the challenges and complexities that lie ahead on our quest for QA excellence.

The Pillars of QA

QA is built upon several core pillars that form the framework for ensuring quality and excellence. These pillars are the cornerstones of the QA process:

- **Testing:** At its core, QA involves testing to identify defects and ensure that a product or process meets specified requirements. Testing can take many forms, from manual testing by human testers to automated testing using specialised tools.

- **Documentation:** Comprehensive documentation is essential in QA. It includes test plans, test cases, test scripts, and detailed records of test results. Documentation not only helps in testing but also aids in traceability and future reference.

- **Process Management:** QA isn't just about testing; it's about managing processes to ensure consistent quality. Process management includes defining and optimising workflows, identifying bottlenecks, and implementing best practices.

- **Continuous Improvement:** QA is an iterative process. Continuous improvement involves learning from past mistakes and successes, refining processes, and striving for ongoing excellence.

- **Risk Management:** QA professionals are risk assessors. They identify potential risks and vulnerabilities, prioritise them, and develop strategies to mitigate or eliminate them.

QA Methodologies

To achieve QA excellence, it's essential to adopt a structured approach. QA methodologies provide the roadmap for conducting QA activities. Some of the most commonly used QA methodologies include:

- **Waterfall:** A traditional, linear approach where each phase of development (e.g., requirements, design, development, testing) is completed before moving to the next.

- **Agile:** An iterative and flexible approach that emphasises collaboration, adaptability, and customer feedback. Agile methodologies include Scrum, Kanban, and Lean.

- **DevOps:** A combination of development and operations that focuses on automation, continuous integration, and continuous delivery (CI/CD) to accelerate software delivery.

- **Six Sigma:** A data-driven methodology that aims to reduce defects and variations in processes to achieve near-perfect quality.

- **Test-Driven Development (TDD):** A development approach where tests are written before code, ensuring that the code meets specific requirements and functions correctly.

Each methodology has its strengths and weaknesses, and the choice of methodology depends on the project's nature, goals, and constraints.

QA Best Practices

While QA methodologies provide the structure, it's the best practices that make QA effective. Here are some QA best practices to keep in mind:

- **Clear Requirements:** Start with well-defined requirements. QA can only ensure that a product meets its requirements if those requirements are clear and unambiguous.

- **Test Planning:** Develop a comprehensive test plan that outlines the scope, objectives, and resources required for testing.

- **Effective Communication:** Foster open communication among team members, stakeholders, and customers to ensure everyone understands QA goals and progress.

- **Test Automation:** Automate repetitive and time-consuming test cases to increase efficiency and coverage.

- **Regression Testing:** Regularly perform regression testing to ensure that new changes haven't introduced unexpected defects.

- **Peer Review:** Encourage peer review of test cases and documentation to catch errors and improve quality.

Conclusion

In the chapters that follow, we'll dive deeper into each of these pillars, methodologies, and best practices. We'll explore the nuts and bolts of QA, from creating test cases to implementing automation and managing risk. By mastering these fundamentals, you'll be well-prepared to embark on the journey towards QA excellence.

So, let's roll up our sleeves and begin building a strong QA foundation. Our quest for excellence continues.

Pause. Introspect. Reflect.

Here are some **Exercise** for Chapter 2, "The Fundamentals of Quality Assurance", that helps you to understand the key concepts and these questions are designed to encourage you to actively engage with the content of this Chapter by applying the concepts to their own experiences, and actively participate in building a strong QA foundation as you progress through next chapter.

Exercise 2.1: Pillars of QA Exploration

Questions:

- Select one of the core pillars of QA mentioned in the chapter (Testing, Documentation, Process Management, Continuous Improvement, Risk Management). Provide a detailed example from your own experience or research that illustrates how this pillar is crucial in ensuring quality.

- Imagine you are in charge of a project that lacks comprehensive documentation. Describe the potential challenges and risks of not having proper documentation in place. How would you address this situation?

Exercise 2.2: QA Methodology Analysis

Questions:

- Research and choose one QA methodology mentioned in the chapter (Waterfall, Agile, DevOps, Six Sigma, Test-Driven Development). Explain the key principles and benefits of this methodology. When would it be most suitable for a project?

- Consider a real or hypothetical project you've worked on. Which QA methodology do you think would have been the most effective for that project, and why?

Exercise 2.3: Best Practices Application

Questions:

- Think about a project you're currently involved in or one you've worked on in the past. How could applying the best practices mentioned in the chapter (e.g., clear requirements, test planning, effective communication) have improved the quality assurance process for that project?

- Identify one area in your current QA process that you believe could benefit from automation. Describe the specific test case or task, and explain how automation could enhance efficiency and effectiveness.

Exercise 2.4: Personal QA Foundation Building

Questions:

- Reflect on the pillars, methodologies, and best practices discussed in the chapter. Which aspect of QA do you feel most confident about, and which aspect do you think requires further development in your own skill set?

- Set a personal goal for enhancing your QA skills based on your reflections. How do you plan to work on this area of improvement?

Exercise 2.5: QA Discussion Forum

Create a discussion forum or group where readers can share their thoughts, experiences, and questions related to the fundamentals of QA. Encourage them to discuss the various pillars, methodologies, and best practices, and facilitate discussions on how these concepts apply to different industries and projects.

*"The only way to do great work is to love what you do." —
Steve Jobs*

Chapter 3

Building Effective Test Cases

Introduction

In our journey towards QA excellence, we've laid the groundwork by understanding the fundamentals of Quality Assurance. Now, it's time to dive into the heart of QA: test cases. Effective test cases are the cornerstone of a successful QA process. They are the roadmaps that guide us in our quest to ensure the quality of products and processes. In this chapter, we'll explore the art and science of crafting test cases that truly make a difference.

The Anatomy of a Test Case

A test case is a detailed document that outlines the steps to be taken, the conditions to be met, and the expected outcomes to be observed during testing. It's a roadmap that guides testers through the validation process. Let's break down the key components of a test case:

- **Test Case ID:** A unique identifier for the test case, often including a project or module prefix.

- **Test Case Title:** A concise, descriptive title that summarises the purpose of the test case.

- **Objective:** A clear statement of the goal or objective of the test case.

- **Preconditions:** The conditions that must be met before the test case can be executed, such as specific data or configurations.

- **Test Steps:** A series of step-by-step instructions that outline the actions to be performed during testing.

- **Expected Results:** The expected outcomes or behaviour that should be observed after executing each test step.

- **Actual Results:** A space to record the actual outcomes observed during testing.

- **Status:** Indicates whether the test case passed, failed, or is pending.

- **Test Case's Category:** To help group the test cases in Positive, Negative, Alternate category

- **Test Case Priority:** To identify higher-priority test cases and focus on those with the most significant potential for fault detection and risk coverage.

- **Notes:** Additional information or context that may be relevant to the test case.

The Art of Test Case Design

Creating effective test cases is both an art and a science. Here are some key principles to keep in mind:

- **Clarity and Simplicity:** Test cases should be easy to understand. Avoid complex language or jargon that may confuse testers.

- **Coverage:** Ensure that your test cases cover all relevant aspects of the product or process. This includes functional requirements, edge cases, and negative scenarios.

- **Independence:** Test cases should be independent of each other, meaning the outcome of one test case should not affect the execution of others.

- **Reusability:** Design test cases with reusability in mind. A well-structured test case can be used across different test cycles and projects.

- **Traceability:** Ensure that test cases are traceable back to the requirements they are validating. This helps maintain alignment with project goals.

Test Data and Test Environments

Effective test cases also require appropriate test data and environments. Test data should represent realistic scenarios and cover a wide range of inputs and conditions. Test environments should mirror the production environment as closely as possible to ensure accurate testing.

Test Case Management Tools

Managing test cases efficiently is crucial to a successful QA process. Test case management tools, such as TestRail,

Jira, Zephyr, XRay, or QATouch can help organise, track, and report on test cases. These tools provide a centralised repository for test cases, making it easier to collaborate with team members and stakeholders.

Continuous Review and Iteration

Test cases are not static documents; they evolve as the product or process changes. It's essential to continuously review and update test cases to ensure they remain relevant and effective. As requirements change or new features are introduced, test cases should be adapted accordingly.

Conclusion

Creating effective test cases is a skill that every QA professional must master on the journey towards QA excellence. Test cases are not just documents; they are the tools that empower us to uncover defects, validate requirements, and deliver high-quality products and processes. In the next chapter, we'll explore the world of test automation and how it can enhance the effectiveness of your test cases.

As you continue your quest for QA excellence, remember that the quality of your test cases reflects the quality of your QA process. So, let's hone our skills in crafting these essential roadmaps and move one step closer to our destination.

Pause. Introspect. Reflect.

Here are some **Exercises** for Chapter 3, "Building Effective Test Cases", these exercises will help you in hands-on activities related to test case creation, review, and management. This will also apply the principles and concepts discussed in the chapter to practical scenarios and develop your skills in crafting effective test cases.

Exercise 3.1: Creating a Test Case

Task: Write a test case for a hypothetical scenario of your choice. Include the following components: Test Case ID, Test Case Title, Objective, Preconditions, Test Steps, Expected Results, Actual Results, Status, Test Case Category, Test Case Priority and Notes. You can choose any scenario, such as testing a login page, a calculator app, or a website registration form. Make sure your test case is clear, concise, and well-structured.

Exercise 3.2: Test Case Review and Improvement

Task: Review a test case written by a peer or colleague (if available) or use one of your own test cases. Evaluate the test case for clarity, coverage, independence, and reusability. Identify any improvements or refinements that could be made to enhance the quality of the test case.

Exercise 3.3: Traceability Exercise

Task: Select a set of test cases from your project or a hypothetical project. For each test case, identify the specific requirement or functionality it is validating. Create a traceability matrix or document that links each test case to its corresponding requirement. Discuss the importance of traceability in ensuring that test cases align with project goals.

Exercise 3.4: Test Data and Environment Planning

Task: Imagine you are responsible for testing a new e-commerce website. Identify the types of test data and conditions you would need to consider when creating test cases. Discuss the importance of realistic test data and a production-like test environment in effective testing.

Exercise 3.5: Test Case Management Tools Exploration

Task: Explore one of the test case management tools mentioned in the chapter (e.g., TestRail, Jira, Zephyr, XRay, QATouch) if available or use a tool you are familiar with. Create a sample test case in the tool and organise it within a test suite or project. Reflect on how using such a tool can streamline test case management and collaboration within a QA team.

Exercise 3.6: Test Case Evolution

Task: Consider a real or hypothetical project where the requirements have changed or new features have been introduced. Discuss how the test cases created for the project would need to be adapted or updated to accommodate these changes. Emphasise the importance of continuous review and iteration in maintaining effective test cases.

"The secret of getting ahead is getting started." — *Mark Twain*

Chapter 4

The Power of Test Automation

Introduction

In our quest for QA excellence, we've learned the art of crafting effective test cases. Now, it's time to explore a game-changing tool in the world of Quality Assurance: test automation. Test automation isn't just a buzzword; it's a strategic approach that can significantly enhance the efficiency and effectiveness of your QA processes. In this chapter, we'll uncover the power of test automation and how it can be harnessed to accelerate your journey towards QA excellence.

Understanding Test Automation

At its core, test automation is the process of using software tools and scripts to perform tests on a system or application. Unlike manual testing, which relies on human testers to execute test cases step by step, test automation involves automating repetitive and time-consuming tasks. This not only saves time but also increases the accuracy and repeatability of testing.

Benefits of Test Automation

Why invest in test automation? Here are some compelling reasons:

- **Speed:** Automated tests can run much faster than manual tests, allowing you to test your software more frequently and thoroughly.

- **Repeatability:** Automated tests execute the same steps consistently, eliminating the variability introduced by human testers.

- **Coverage:** Automation enables you to cover a broader range of test cases, including those that are tedious or impossible to execute manually.

- **Regression Testing:** Automated tests are ideal for regression testing, ensuring that new changes don't introduce previously fixed defects.

- **Continuous Integration:** In Agile and DevOps environments, automated tests can be seamlessly integrated into the continuous integration/ continuous delivery (CI/CD) pipeline.

Selecting the Right Automation Tools

Choosing the right automation tools is a crucial step in your automation journey. Some popular test automation tools include Selenium, Appium, JUnit, TestNG, Playright and many more. The choice of tools depends on factors like the technology stack of your application, your team's expertise, and the specific testing needs of your project.

Designing a Robust Automation Framework

Successful test automation requires a well-designed automation framework. An automation framework provides a structured approach for creating, organising, and running automated tests. Key components of an automation framework include:

- **Test scripts:** The actual test cases written in the chosen automation tool's scripting language.

- **Test data:** Input data required for the test cases.

- **Reporting:** Tools for generating detailed test reports.

- **Configuration management:** Handling different test environments and configurations.

- **Logging and debugging:** Tools and techniques for troubleshooting and debugging test failures.

Balancing Manual and Automated Testing

While automation is powerful, it's not a silver bullet. There will always be scenarios where manual testing is more appropriate. Balancing manual and automated testing is key to a successful QA strategy. Manual testing is especially valuable for exploratory testing, usability testing, and ad-hoc testing.

Challenges and Pitfalls of Test Automation

Test automation isn't without challenges. Some common pitfalls to watch out for are:

- **High Initial Setup Costs:** Developing and maintaining automation scripts can be resource-intensive initially.

- **Maintenance Overhead:** As the application evolves, automation scripts may require frequent updates to remain relevant.

- **False Positives:** Automated tests can sometimes produce false-positive results, requiring manual intervention to verify issues.

- **Selectivity:** Not all tests are suitable for automation. Identifying the right candidates for automation is crucial.

Conclusion

Test automation is a powerful tool in the pursuit of QA excellence. When used strategically, it can accelerate testing cycles, increase coverage, and improve overall product quality. However, it's essential to approach automation with careful planning, selecting the right tools, and balancing it with manual testing where necessary.

As we continue our journey towards QA excellence, keep in mind that test automation is a valuable ally but not a substitute for the critical thinking and creativity that human testers bring to the table. In the next chapter, we'll explore the crucial aspect of managing risk in QA—a skill that complements both manual and automated testing.

So, let's harness the power of automation and continue our quest for excellence in Quality Assurance.

Pause. Introspect. Reflect.

Here are some **Exercises** for Chapter 4, "The Power of Test Automation", these exercises will encourage you to explore test automation tools, gain practical experience in creating automated test scripts, and consider the strategic aspects of implementing automation in their projects. It will also foster discussions and reflections on the challenges and benefits of test automation in the context of QA excellence.

Exercise 4.1: Tool Selection and Evaluation

Task: Research and evaluate a test automation tool of your choice (e.g., Selenium, Appium, JUnit, TestNG, Playright). Identify its key features, advantages, and limitations. Create a summary report highlighting why you would or wouldn't choose this tool for a hypothetical testing project.

Exercise 4.2: Automated Test Case Creation

Task: Select a simple scenario or feature from a real or hypothetical project. Write an automated test script using your chosen automation tool to test this scenario. Include necessary test data and assertions to validate the expected behaviour. Execute the script and document the results.

Exercise 4.3: Automation Framework Components

Task: Imagine you are tasked with designing an automation framework for your project. Create a high-level diagram or outline of your proposed framework, including components like test scripts, test data, reporting, and configuration management. Explain how each component contributes to the overall framework's effectiveness.

Exercise 4.4: Test Automation ROI Analysis

Task: Conduct a cost-benefit analysis of test automation for a hypothetical project. Estimate the initial setup costs, ongoing maintenance costs, and the expected benefits in terms of time saved, increased coverage, and reduced human error. Determine whether automation is justified for this project and explain your reasoning.

Exercise 4.5: Identifying Manual Testing Scenarios

Task: List five scenarios or types of testing that you believe are better suited for manual testing rather than automation. Explain why automation may not be the ideal choice for these scenarios, taking into account factors like complexity, exploration, and usability.

Exercise 4.6: Test Automation Challenges Discussion

Task: Engage in a group discussion or forum with fellow readers or colleagues to share experiences and insights regarding the challenges and pitfalls of test automation. Discuss strategies for overcoming these challenges and share best practices for successful test automation implementation.

"The most powerful tool in testing is the human brain." —
James Bach

Chapter 5

Managing Risk in QA

Introduction

Risk management is a critical aspect of Quality Assurance (QA). As we continue our journey towards QA excellence, we'll delve into the world of risk management and its vital role in ensuring the quality and reliability of products and processes. In this chapter, we'll explore how to identify, assess, prioritise, and mitigate risks effectively in your QA endeavours.

Understanding Risk in QA

In the context of QA, risk refers to the possibility of something going wrong or not meeting expectations. This "something" could be a defect in the software, a delay in the project schedule, a security breach, or any other event that could have a negative impact on quality, cost, or timelines.

The Risk Management Process

Effective risk management in QA involves a structured process:

- **Identification:** The first step is to identify potential risks. This can be done through brainstorming sessions, reviewing project documentation, or drawing from past experiences. The goal is to create a comprehensive list of possible risks.

- **Assessment:** Once risks are identified, they need to be assessed. Assessment involves evaluating the likelihood of each risk occurring and the potential impact it could have on the project. Risks are often assessed using a simple scale, such as low, medium, or high.

- **Prioritisation:** Not all risks are equally important. Prioritisation involves ranking risks based on their severity and likelihood. High-priority risks require immediate attention and mitigation.

- **Mitigation:** Mitigation strategies are put in place to address high-priority risks. These strategies could involve changes to the project plan, additional testing, security measures, or contingency plans.

- **Monitoring:** Risk management is an ongoing process. Risks should be monitored throughout the project to ensure that mitigation strategies are effective and to identify any new risks that may arise.

Types of Risks in QA

QA professionals should be aware of various types of risks, including:

- **Technical Risks:** These relate to defects and vulnerabilities in the software or product being tested. Technical risks can lead to functionality failures or security breaches.

- **Schedule Risks:** Delays in testing or development can impact project timelines. Identifying and mitigating schedule risks is essential to meeting deadlines.

- **Resource Risks:** Insufficient resources, such as not having enough skilled testers or suitable test environments, can hinder QA efforts.

- **Cost Risks:** Unexpected expenses related to QA, such as additional testing tools or equipment, can affect project budgets.

- **Operational Risks:** These encompass risks associated with how the software or product will be used in the real world. This includes factors like user errors, data entry mistakes, and external threats.

Risk Mitigation Strategies

Mitigating risks in QA involves developing and implementing strategies to reduce the likelihood and impact of identified risks. Common risk mitigation strategies include:

- **Test Planning:** Comprehensive test planning can help identify and address technical and schedule risks early in the project.

- **Security Measures:** Implementing security testing and measures to protect against data breaches and cyber threats.

- **Test Automation:** Automation can help mitigate resource and schedule risks by speeding up testing processes.

- **Contingency Planning:** Preparing contingency plans for high-priority risks, such as backup testing environments or alternative project schedules.

Continuous Risk Assessment

Risk management is not a one-time activity; it's a continuous process. As the project progresses and circumstances change, new risks may emerge, and the severity of existing risks may fluctuate. Regularly revisiting and updating your risk assessment is crucial to effective risk management.

Conclusion

Managing risk in QA is not about eliminating all risks but about identifying and mitigating the most critical ones. By systematically addressing risks throughout the QA process, you can enhance the quality, reliability, and success of your projects.

As we continue our journey towards QA excellence, remember that risk management is a skill that requires constant vigilance and adaptability. In the next chapter, we'll explore the world of metrics and reporting in QA—a vital aspect of assessing project health and quality.

So, let's continue to embrace risk management as a valuable tool in our pursuit of QA excellence.

Pause. Introspect. Reflect.

Here are some **Exercises** for Chapter 5, "Managing Risk in QA", that will help you to actively apply risk management principles to QA scenarios, prioritise risks, develop mitigation strategies, and adapt to changing circumstances. By doing so, you will gain practical experience in managing risk in the context of Quality Assurance.

Exercise 5.1: Identifying Risks

Task: Select a hypothetical or real QA project (e.g., testing a mobile app, a website, or a software product). List at least five potential risks that could affect the success of the project. For each risk, provide a brief description and explain its potential impact on the project.

Exercise 5.2: Risk Assessment

Task: Take the list of risks you generated in *Exercise 1* and assess each risk's likelihood and impact using a simple scale (e.g., low, medium, high). Rank the risks based on their overall risk level (the product of likelihood and impact). Discuss which risks are most critical and require immediate attention.

Exercise 5.3: Risk Mitigation Strategies

Task: Select one of the high-priority risks identified in *Exercise 2*. Develop a risk mitigation strategy for that specific risk. Describe the actions you would take to reduce the likelihood and impact of the risk. Consider whether changes to the project plan, additional testing, or contingency plans are necessary.

Exercise 5.4: Continuous Risk Monitoring

Task: Imagine you are in the middle of a QA project, and circumstances have changed. Some risks have evolved, and new ones have emerged. Create a plan for how you would conduct a mid-project risk assessment. Explain how you would identify and prioritise these new or evolving risks and adapt your risk mitigation strategies.

Exercise 5.5: Operational Risk Analysis

Task: Think about the operational risks associated with the software or product being tested. Develop a scenario or case study where operational risks could come into play. Describe how these risks could affect end-users or the system's overall performance. Discuss possible mitigation strategies to address these operational risks.

Exercise 5.6: Risk Management Discussion Forum

Task: Set up a discussion forum or group where readers can share their experiences and insights related to risk management in QA. Encourage them to discuss challenges they've faced, successful risk mitigation strategies they've employed, and any lessons learned. Facilitate a discussion on the importance of continuous risk assessment.

"Quality is not an act, it is a habit." — Aristotle

Chapter 6

Metrics and Reporting in QA

Introduction

In our journey towards QA excellence, we've explored the critical aspects of test case design, automation, and risk management. Now, let's shift our focus to another essential component of Quality Assurance: metrics and reporting. Metrics provide us with valuable insights into the quality of our products and processes, helping us make informed decisions and drive continuous improvement. In this chapter, we'll delve into the world of QA metrics and reporting and discover their role in achieving QA excellence.

The Importance of QA Metrics

Why are metrics essential in QA? Metrics provide quantifiable data that allows us to assess the effectiveness of our QA efforts, track progress, and make data-driven decisions. They offer several key benefits:

- **Visibility:** Metrics provide visibility into the quality and performance of a project, allowing stakeholders to understand its current state.

- **Early Detection:** Metrics can help identify issues and defects early in the development cycle, allowing for timely corrective action.

- **Performance Evaluation:** Metrics enable the evaluation of QA teams and processes, helping identify areas for improvement.

- **Benchmarking:** Metrics provide a basis for benchmarking against industry standards and best practices.

Types of QA Metrics

QA metrics can encompass various aspects of the QA process. Some common types of QA metrics include:

- **Defect Metrics:** These metrics track defects found during testing, including their severity, frequency, ageing and resolution times.

- **Test Coverage Metrics:** Test coverage metrics measure the extent to which a product or application has been tested. This includes requirements coverage and code coverage.

- **Test Execution Metrics:** These metrics provide insights into test execution progress, including the number of test cases executed, passed, and failed.

- **Test Automation Metrics:** Metrics related to automated testing, such as the percentage of test cases automated, automation test pass rate, and automation test execution time.

- **Test Cycle Metrics:** Metrics related to the entire testing cycle, including the duration of test cycles and the number of cycles required.

- **Resource Metrics:** Metrics related to QA resources, including team productivity, resource allocation, and testing effort.

- **Defect Density:** The number of defects per unit of code or requirements, which helps identify quality hotspots.

Selecting Relevant Metrics

Not all metrics are equally valuable. It's essential to choose metrics that align with project goals and objectives. Metrics should be relevant, actionable, and aligned with the project's critical success factors. For example, if a project's goal is to improve software stability, metrics related to defect density and regression test coverage might be more relevant than metrics related to test execution speed.

Creating Meaningful Reports

Effective reporting is a key component of QA metrics. Reports should be clear, concise, and targeted to the audience. When creating reports, consider the following:

- **Audience:** Tailor reports to the needs and interests of different stakeholders, such as project managers, developers, and executives.

- **Frequency:** Determine how often reports should be generated and distributed. Regular reporting ensures that project status is up to date.

- **Visualisations:** Visual elements, such as charts and graphs, can make data more accessible and understandable.

- **Actionability:** Reports should provide actionable insights and recommendations for improvement.

Continuous Improvement

QA metrics and reporting are not static. They should evolve as the project progresses and as goals and priorities change. Regularly review and assess the effectiveness of your chosen metrics, and adjust them as needed to better serve the project's objectives.

Conclusion

QA metrics and reporting are powerful tools in the pursuit of QA excellence. By effectively tracking and analysing data, we gain valuable insights that can drive improvements in product quality, process efficiency, and team performance. Metrics and reports not only provide a snapshot of the current state of a project but also pave the way for informed decision-making and continuous improvement.

As we continue our journey, remember that the value of metrics lies not only in the numbers themselves but in the actions they inspire. In the next chapter, we'll explore the human element of QA: team dynamics and collaboration—a critical factor in achieving QA excellence.

So, let's harness the power of metrics and reporting to propel ourselves closer to our goal of QA excellence.

Pause. Introspect. Reflect.

Here are some **Exercises** for Chapter 6, "Metrics and Reporting in QA", these exercises will get you hands-on activities related to metric selection, report creation, benchmark analysis, and continuous improvement in the context of QA metrics and reporting. By actively participating in these exercises, you can apply the concepts discussed in the chapter and gain practical experience in using metrics to drive QA excellence.

Exercise 6.1: Metric Selection

Task: Imagine you are working on a QA project for a mobile application. Identify at least three specific metrics that you believe would be valuable for tracking the quality of the application. Explain why you selected these metrics and how they align with project goals.

Exercise 6.2: Report Creation

Task: Select one of the metrics identified in Exercise 1. Create a sample report that presents data for this metric over a specific time frame (e.g., weekly or monthly). Include visualisations such as charts or graphs to illustrate trends. Write a brief summary of the insights and actions that can be derived from this report.

Exercise 6.3: Metric Evaluation

Task: Research industry benchmarks or standards for one of the metrics commonly used in QA (e.g., defect density, test coverage). Compare your project's performance in this metric to the industry benchmark. Discuss the implications of this comparison and whether there are opportunities for improvement.

Exercise 6.4: Audience-Targeted Reporting

Task: Imagine you are responsible for reporting QA metrics to two different audiences: project managers and developers. Create two distinct reports for each audience using the same set of metrics. Adapt the language and content to cater to the specific interests and needs of each group.

Exercise 6.5: Continuous Improvement Plan

Task: Reflect on the metrics and reporting practices used in your current or past QA projects. Identify one area where you believe improvements can be made in terms of metric selection, reporting clarity, or actionability. Develop a plan for implementing this improvement in a future project.

Exercise 6.6: Peer Review and Feedback

Task: Exchange your sample reports created in Exercise 2 with a peer or colleague. Provide feedback to each other on the clarity, visual appeal, and actionability of the reports. Discuss how the reports could be further improved to effectively communicate insights.

"Quality is never an accident; it is always the result of intelligent effort." — *John Ruskin*

Chapter 7

The Human Element: QA Team Dynamics

Introduction

As we've explored various aspects of Quality Assurance (QA) on our journey towards excellence, we've encountered tools, processes, and methodologies. Now, let's shift our focus to the human element—the individuals who work together to make QA successful.

In this chapter, we'll explore the dynamics of QA teams and the critical role of collaboration, communication, and teamwork in achieving QA excellence.

The Importance of Team Dynamics in QA

QA is not a solitary endeavour but a collaborative one. QA teams are composed of diverse individuals with unique skills, experiences, and perspectives. The effectiveness of these teams hinges on their ability to work cohesively towards a common goal: ensuring the quality of the product or process under test.

Key Elements of QA Team Dynamics

- **Clear Roles and Responsibilities:** Each team member should have a clearly defined role and set of responsibilities. This clarity prevents confusion and overlaps in tasks.

- **Effective Communication:** Open, transparent, and timely communication is essential in QA teams. It ensures that everyone is informed, aligned, and able to address issues proactively.

- **Collaboration:** QA teams collaborate not only with each other but also with developers, product managers, and other stakeholders. Collaboration promotes the sharing of knowledge and ideas, leading to better testing strategies.

- **Diversity and Inclusion:** Embracing diversity in QA teams fosters innovation and brings a range of perspectives to problem-solving. Inclusion ensures that all team members feel valued and heard.

- **Adaptability:** QA teams need to adapt to changing project requirements, timelines, and priorities. An adaptable team is more resilient and responsive to challenges.

The Role of Leadership in QA Teams

Leadership within a QA team is crucial for setting a positive tone and guiding team members toward success. Effective QA leaders:

- Provide clear direction and vision for the team.

- Foster a culture of continuous improvement and learning.

- Encourage open communication and feedback.

- Empower team members to take ownership of their work.

- Recognize and celebrate achievements.

Challenges and Strategies for Remote and Distributed QA Teams

In today's globalised world, many QA teams work remotely or are distributed across different locations. While remote work offers flexibility, it can present challenges in team dynamics. Strategies for addressing these challenges include:

- Leveraging collaboration tools and communication platforms.

- Setting clear expectations and guidelines for remote work.

- Scheduling regular team meetings and check-ins.

- Encouraging virtual team-building activities.

Conflict Resolution in QA Teams

Conflict is a natural part of team dynamics. It can arise from differences in opinions, approaches, or priorities. Effective conflict resolution involves:

- Acknowledging and addressing conflicts promptly.

- Encouraging open dialogue to understand each party's perspective.

- Finding common ground and mutually agreeable solutions.

- Learning from conflicts to prevent similar issues in the future.

Conclusion

In the journey towards QA excellence, never underestimate the power of effective team dynamics. QA teams are more than just the sum of their individual members; they are collective forces for quality and excellence. By nurturing collaboration, communication, and teamwork, QA teams can overcome challenges, adapt to change, and deliver exceptional results.

As we continue our quest, remember that while tools and processes are essential, it's the people behind them who truly drive QA excellence. In the next chapter, we'll explore how QA fits into Agile and DevOps environments, where collaboration and teamwork are central to success.

So, let's celebrate the human element in QA and strive for excellence through effective team dynamics.

Pause. Introspect. Reflect.

Here are some **Exercises** for Chapter 7, "The Human Element: QA Team Dynamics", aimed to engage you in hands-on activities that explore the dynamics of QA teams, effective communication, conflict resolution, leadership, and remote teamwork. By actively participating in these exercises, you can gain practical insights into fostering effective team dynamics in the context of Quality Assurance.

Exercise 7.1: Team Roles and Responsibilities

Task: Imagine you are part of a QA team or leading one. Create a document that outlines the roles and responsibilities of each team member. Ensure that roles are clear, and responsibilities do not overlap. Share this document with your team and encourage feedback and adjustments as needed.

Exercise 7.2: Effective Communication Workshop

Task: Organise a virtual workshop or meeting with your QA team (or a group of colleagues). Discuss the importance of effective communication within a QA team. Explore best practices for improving communication, such as using collaboration tools, setting clear expectations, and encouraging open dialogue. Share personal experiences and tips for overcoming communication challenges.

Exercise 7.3: Conflict Resolution Scenario

Task: Present a hypothetical conflict scenario to your QA team or a group of colleagues. This scenario could involve differences in testing approaches, priorities, or resource allocation. Encourage team members to engage in a role-play exercise to resolve the conflict. Afterward, discuss the strategies used for conflict resolution and identify lessons learned.

Exercise 7.4: Leadership Skills Assessment

Task: Encourage team members to assess their leadership skills and qualities. Provide a list of leadership traits or competencies (e.g., communication, adaptability, empowerment). Ask team members to rate themselves on each trait and reflect on areas where they can improve their leadership within the QA team. Encourage a discussion on leadership development strategies.

Exercise 7.5: Virtual Team-Building Activity

Task: If your QA team works remotely or in a distributed fashion, plan a virtual team-building activity. This could be a virtual escape room, a trivia quiz, or a collaborative problem-solving exercise. The goal is to strengthen team bonds, promote collaboration, and have fun while working together virtually.

Exercise 7.6: Leadership Role Play

Task: Organise a role-play activity where team members take turns assuming leadership roles within the QA team. Each participant can lead a team meeting or discussion on a specific topic. This exercise allows team members to practise leadership skills, gain experience in guiding discussions, and receive feedback from peers.

"The difference between ordinary and extraordinary is that little extra." — Jimmy Johnson

Chapter 8

Adapting to Agile and DevOps Environments

Introduction

In our journey towards QA excellence, we've explored the fundamentals of Quality Assurance, test automation, risk management, metrics and reporting, team dynamics, and more. Now, we step into the dynamic world of Agile and DevOps, where speed, collaboration, and continuous improvement are the norm. In this chapter, we'll learn how to adapt our QA practices to thrive in Agile and DevOps environments and play a pivotal role in delivering high-quality software at speed.

The Agile Revolution

Agile methodologies have transformed the software development landscape. Agile promotes iterative and collaborative development, breaking down long development cycles into smaller, manageable increments called sprints or iterations. Key principles of Agile include:

- **Customer Collaboration:** Actively involving customers and stakeholders in the development process to ensure alignment with their needs and expectations.

- **Iterative Development:** Breaking down project work into smaller, functional pieces, which are continuously developed, tested, and delivered.

- **Embracing Change:** Welcoming changes in requirements, even late in the development cycle, to remain flexible and responsive.

The Role of QA in Agile

In Agile environments, QA takes on a more integrated and continuous role:

- **Test Early and Often:** QA begins in the early stages of development and continues throughout each sprint. Testers collaborate closely with developers to identify and resolve issues as they arise.

- **Test Automation:** Automation plays a vital role in Agile QA. Automated tests are continuously executed to ensure that new code changes do not introduce regressions.

- **User Stories and Acceptance Criteria:** QA professionals work with product owners and stakeholders to define clear user stories and acceptance criteria that drive development and testing efforts.

- **Continuous Feedback:** Agile emphasises continuous feedback loops. QA provides feedback on the quality of work delivered in each sprint, helping the team adapt and improve.

DevOps: Bridging the Gap Between Development and Operations

DevOps is an extension of Agile principles, focusing on the collaboration between development and operations teams to streamline the software delivery process. Key DevOps practices include:

- **Continuous Integration (CI):** Frequent integration of code changes into a shared repository, followed by automated testing and deployment.

- **Continuous Delivery (CD):** The ability to automatically build, test, and deploy code changes to production or staging environments.

- **Infrastructure as Code (IaC):** Treating infrastructure configuration as code, enabling automated provisioning and management of resources.

The Role of QA in DevOps

QA in DevOps extends beyond traditional testing:

- **Continuous Testing:** Automated tests are integrated into the CI/CD pipeline, ensuring that code changes are tested continuously.

- **Shift-Left Testing:** QA is involved early in the development process, identifying and addressing potential issues before they reach production.

- **Infrastructure Testing:** QA may be responsible for testing infrastructure configurations, ensuring that the infrastructure is reliable and consistent.

- **Monitoring and Feedback:** QA monitors production environments for issues and provides feedback for continuous improvement.

Challenges and Strategies

Transitioning to Agile and DevOps can be challenging. Here are some common challenges and strategies to overcome them:

- **Culture Change:** Encourage a culture of collaboration, transparency, and continuous learning.

- **Skill Development:** Invest in training and development to equip QA professionals with the necessary skills for Agile and DevOps practices.

- **Tool Selection:** Choose tools that support automation, collaboration, and continuous testing.

- **Communication:** Foster clear and open communication between teams to prevent silos and ensure alignment.

Conclusion

Adapting to Agile and DevOps environments requires a shift in mindset, practices, and culture. As QA professionals, our role is to be adaptable, collaborative, and continuously focused on delivering high-quality software.

In our pursuit of QA excellence, we must embrace the principles of Agile and DevOps and use them as catalysts for innovation and continuous improvement. In the next chapter, we'll explore how AI and machine learning are shaping the future of QA—a future where automation, intelligence, and human expertise work hand in hand.

So, let's adapt, collaborate, and thrive in the fast-paced world of Agile and DevOps as we continue our quest for excellence.

Pause. Introspect. Reflect.

Here are some **Exercises** for Chapter 8, "Adapting to Agile and DevOps Environments", that help you to understand and apply the concepts related to Agile and DevOps in the context of Quality Assurance. By engaging in these activities, one can gain a deeper understanding of how QA functions in Agile and DevOps environments and how to adapt their practices for success.

Exercise 8.1: Agile Scrum Simulation

Task: Organise a simulation of an Agile Scrum development cycle. Assign roles such as Scrum Master, Product Owner, Developers, and QA Testers. Create a backlog of user stories, and go through sprint planning, daily stand-ups, sprint review, and retrospective meetings. Encourage participants to experience the Agile process firsthand and discuss the challenges and benefits.

Exercise 8.2: Continuous Integration and Continuous Delivery (CI/CD) Pipeline Setup

Task: Set up a simplified CI/CD pipeline for a sample project. Include stages for code integration, automated testing, and deployment to a staging environment. Demonstrate how code changes are automatically built, tested, and deployed as part of the pipeline. Discuss the importance of QA's role in ensuring the pipeline's quality gates.

Exercise 8.3: Infrastructure as Code (IaC) Testing

Task: Introduce participants to Infrastructure as Code (IaC) concepts and tools (e.g., Terraform or AWS CloudFormation). Provide a sample IaC script for provisioning infrastructure resources. Ask participants to review and test the script for potential issues or improvements. Highlight the role of QA in verifying infrastructure changes.

Exercise 8.4: Collaboration Workshop

Task: Organise a workshop that focuses on improving collaboration between development, operations, and QA teams in a DevOps context. Use real or hypothetical scenarios to identify areas where collaboration can be enhanced. Encourage participants to brainstorm and implement strategies for better teamwork.

Exercise 8.5: DevOps Tool Evaluation

Task: Assign teams or individuals to research and evaluate DevOps tools (e.g., Jenkins, Docker, Kubernetes) that support CI/CD and automation. Have them present their findings, including features, benefits, and potential challenges. Discuss how the selected tools can enhance QA processes in a DevOps environment.

Exercise 8.6: Transition Plan for Agile/DevOps Adoption

Task: Ask participants to create a transition plan outlining how their QA team would transition from traditional development practices to Agile and DevOps. Include steps, timelines, resource allocation, and expected outcomes. Discuss the challenges and opportunities presented by the transition.

"Testing is not about finding defects; it's about preventing defects leaking to production." — Shree

Chapter 9

QA in the Era of AI and Machine Learning

Introduction

As our journey towards QA excellence continues, we find ourselves at the forefront of technological innovation. In this chapter, we'll explore the exciting and transformative landscape of AI (Artificial Intelligence) and ML (Machine Learning) in Quality Assurance. These emerging technologies are reshaping how we test and validate software, opening new possibilities and challenges that we must embrace to remain at the cutting edge of QA.

The Promise of AI and Machine Learning in QA

AI and ML have the potential to revolutionise the way we approach Quality Assurance:

- **Automated Testing:** AI-powered testing tools can autonomously create, execute, and analyse test cases, significantly reducing manual testing efforts.

- **Test Case Generation:** ML algorithms can generate test cases based on code analysis, requirements, and historical test data, increasing test coverage.

- **Defect Prediction:** ML models can predict where defects are most likely to occur in the code, helping prioritise testing efforts.

- **Log Analysis:** AI can analyse logs and error messages to identify anomalies and potential issues, improving troubleshooting.

- **Visual Testing:** AI can perform visual testing by comparing expected and actual UI layouts and elements, ensuring consistency across platforms.

Challenges in Implementing AI and ML in QA

While the potential benefits are immense, integrating AI and ML into QA comes with challenges:

- **Data Quality:** ML models require high-quality training data. Ensuring data accuracy and relevance is crucial.

- **Skill Gaps:** Teams may require training to understand and work with AI and ML technologies effectively.

- **Integration:** Integrating AI-powered tools into existing workflows and processes can be complex.

- **Cost:** Implementing AI and ML solutions may involve significant upfront costs.

Use Cases for AI and ML in QA

Let's explore some practical applications of AI and ML in QA:

- **Test Automation:** AI-driven test automation tools can learn and adapt to application changes, reducing maintenance efforts.

- **Predictive Analytics:** ML models can predict which test cases are most likely to fail, allowing teams to focus on high-risk areas.

- **Natural Language Processing (NLP):** NLP can analyse user feedback and comments to identify common issues and sentiment trends.

- **Anomaly Detection:** AI algorithms can detect unusual behaviour in applications, such as security breaches or performance bottlenecks.

Human-AI Collaboration

AI and ML are not here to replace QA professionals but to augment their capabilities:

- **AI-Assisted Testing:** QA professionals can leverage AI-powered tools to improve test case design, execution, and analysis.

- **Quality Control:** Humans are still essential for subjective assessments, usability testing, and exploratory testing.

- **Ethical Considerations:** QA teams must consider ethical implications when using AI, such as data privacy and bias.

Preparing for the Future of QA

As we navigate the evolving landscape of AI and ML in QA, here are some steps to consider:

- **Education and Training:** Invest in training to equip QA professionals with the skills needed to work with AI and ML technologies effectively.

- **Pilot Projects:** Start with small, controlled pilot projects to assess the feasibility and benefits of AI and ML in your QA processes.

- **Collaboration:** Foster collaboration between QA teams and data science teams to leverage expertise and resources effectively.

- **Ethical Guidelines:** Develop ethical guidelines and policies for AI usage in QA to ensure responsible and unbiased testing.

Conclusion

AI and Machine Learning represent the next frontier in Quality Assurance. Embracing these technologies offers the potential for more efficient, effective, and intelligent QA processes. However, it's essential to approach AI and ML integration with careful planning, ethical considerations, and a commitment to continuous learning.

As we continue our journey towards QA excellence, let's harness the power of AI and Machine Learning to augment our capabilities and remain at the forefront of innovation in Quality Assurance. In the final chapter, we'll reflect on the continuous quest for excellence and the mindset needed to thrive in an ever-evolving QA landscape.

So, let's begin on this exciting journey into the future of QA and the limitless possibilities it holds.

Pause. Introspect. Reflect.

In this chapter, we've explored the transformative potential of AI and Machine Learning in Quality Assurance. These technologies promise to reshape how we approach testing and validation, offering automation, predictive capabilities, and advanced analysis. However, they also come with challenges related to data quality, skill gaps, integration, and cost.

As we prepare to embrace the future of QA, it's essential to reflect on the following questions:

- How can AI and ML technologies be integrated into your organisation's QA processes to maximise their benefits?

- What specific QA tasks or areas do you believe could benefit the most from AI and ML applications?

- What challenges or concerns do you foresee when implementing AI and ML in your QA practice, and how can you address them proactively?

Discussion Questions:

- How do you envision the role of QA professionals evolving as AI and ML become more integrated into QA processes?

- What ethical considerations should QA teams keep in mind when using AI and ML technologies for testing?

- Can you share examples of successful AI or ML implementations in QA, or any lessons learned from such projects?

- How can organisations ensure that AI and ML solutions used in QA are transparent, accountable, and free from bias?

"The best testers are those who never give up, who continuously learn, adapt and who embrace the challenges of quality assurance." — Shree

Chapter 10

The Quest for Continuous QA Excellence

Introduction

As we reach the final chapter of our journey towards QA excellence, it's time to reflect on the path we've travelled, the knowledge we've gained, and the mindset needed to thrive in the ever-evolving landscape of Quality Assurance. QA excellence is not a destination but a continuous quest—a commitment to continuous learning, improvement, and innovation. In this chapter, we'll explore the principles and practices that underpin this quest for excellence.

Embracing a Growth Mindset

At the heart of QA excellence is a growth mindset—a belief that abilities and intelligence can be developed through dedication and hard work. QA professionals who embrace a growth mindset are more likely to:

- Seek out opportunities for learning and skill development.

- Embrace challenges as opportunities for growth.

- Persist in the face of setbacks and failures.

- See feedback and criticism as valuable sources of improvement.

Continuous Learning and Skill Development

QA is a rapidly evolving field. To achieve excellence, QA professionals must commit to lifelong learning:

- **Stay Informed:** Keep up with industry trends, emerging technologies, and best practices through blogs, forums, conferences, and online courses.

- **Certifications:** Consider pursuing relevant certifications to validate your expertise and knowledge in QA.

- **Experiment and Innovate:** Don't be afraid to experiment with new tools and methodologies. Innovation often arises from exploring uncharted territory.

Effective Communication and Collaboration

Effective communication and collaboration are the cornerstones of QA excellence:

- **Clear Communication:** Communicate clearly and openly with team members, stakeholders, and other departments to ensure alignment and transparency.

- **Collaborative Spirit:** Embrace collaboration with developers, product managers, designers, and other stakeholders to foster a culture of shared responsibility for quality.

Adaptability and Resilience

In the dynamic world of software development, adaptability and resilience are essential qualities:

- **Adapt to Change:** Be open to change, whether it's adopting new tools, processes, or methodologies, to meet evolving project requirements.

- **Resilience:** Bounce back from challenges and setbacks with resilience. Use failures as opportunities for learning and improvement.

QA Process Improvement

Excellence in QA is not static; it's a journey of continuous improvement:

- **Process Review:** Regularly review and assess your QA processes and methodologies for areas of improvement.

- **Feedback Loops:** Establish feedback loops within your team to identify issues early and iterate on solutions.

- **Metrics and Reporting:** Leverage QA metrics and reporting to assess the effectiveness of your processes and drive improvements.

Mentorship and Knowledge Sharing

Sharing knowledge and mentoring others is a powerful way to contribute to QA excellence:

- **Mentorship:** Mentor junior QA professionals and help them grow in their roles.

- **Knowledge Sharing:** Contribute to the QA community by sharing your insights, experiences, and lessons learned.

Ethical Considerations

QA professionals must consider ethical implications in their work, such as data privacy, security, and the responsible use of AI and ML:

- **Ethical Guidelines:** Develop and adhere to ethical guidelines to ensure that QA practices align with ethical principles and industry standards.

Conclusion

QA excellence is not a final destination; it's an ongoing quest fueled by a growth mindset, continuous learning, effective communication, and a commitment to improvement. In the ever-evolving landscape of software quality, QA professionals must embrace change, adapt to new challenges, and strive for excellence in every aspect of their work.

As we conclude this journey, remember that excellence is not a destination but a mindset—a mindset that drives us to be the best QA professionals we can be. Let's continue to learn, adapt, and grow as we navigate the ever-changing world of Quality Assurance.

So, let's start on this continuous quest for QA excellence with renewed vigor and enthusiasm, knowing that the journey itself is the destination.

"It is not a test that finds a bug but it is a human that finds a bug and a test plays a role in helping the human find it."
— Pradeep Soundararajan

Key Takeaways: Reflecting the Journey

- **Quality Assurance (QA) Excellence is a Continuous Quest:** QA excellence is not a destination but an ongoing journey of improvement, learning, and adaptation.

- **Effective Test Case Design:** Well-designed test cases are the foundation of successful QA. They should be clear, comprehensive, and aligned with project goals.

- **The Power of Test Automation:** Test automation accelerates testing, improves repeatability, and allows for broader test coverage. However, it should be used strategically and balanced with manual testing when necessary.

- **Risk Management in QA:** Identifying, assessing, prioritising, and mitigating risks is essential for maintaining product quality and project success.

- **Metrics and Reporting:** QA metrics provide valuable insights into project quality and progress. Effective reporting helps stakeholders make informed decisions and drive continuous improvement.

- **Team Dynamics and Collaboration:** Effective collaboration, clear communication, and strong teamwork are crucial for QA success. Leadership plays a pivotal role in setting a positive team tone.

- **Adapting to Agile and DevOps:** Embracing Agile and DevOps methodologies requires adaptability, collaboration, and a shift in mindset. QA professionals become integral parts of cross-functional teams.

- **AI and Machine Learning in QA:** AI and ML technologies offer opportunities for automation, predictive analytics, and enhanced testing capabilities. They should be embraced responsibly and with a focus on ethical considerations.

- **A Growth Mindset is Key:** QA professionals should cultivate a growth mindset, embracing challenges, learning from failures, and continuously improving their skills and processes.

- **Ethical Considerations:** Ethical guidelines in QA are crucial, particularly when handling sensitive data and using emerging technologies like AI and ML.

- **Continuous Improvement:** QA processes should be regularly reviewed, and feedback loops should be established to drive continuous improvement.

- **Mentorship and Knowledge Sharing:** Sharing knowledge and mentoring others contribute to the growth of QA professionals and the QA community.

- **QA Excellence is a Mindset:** Excellence in QA is not just about tools and processes; it's a mindset that drives professionals to deliver high-quality software and continuously strive for improvement.

Appendix A:
Glossary of QA Terms

In the world of Quality Assurance (QA), various terms and acronyms are commonly used. This glossary provides definitions and explanations to help readers better understand QA terminology.

- **Acceptance Testing:** A phase of testing where the product is evaluated against predefined criteria to determine if it meets the requirements and is ready for release.

- **Agile:** A methodology for software development that emphasises iterative development, collaboration, and customer feedback.

- **Automation Testing:** The use of automated scripts and tools to perform tests on software applications, often used to speed up repetitive testing tasks.

- **Bug:** An issue or defect in a software application that causes it to behave in an unintended or undesirable way.

- **Continuous Integration (CI):** A development practice where code changes are frequently integrated into a shared repository and automatically built and tested.

- **Defect:** A variation between expected and actual results in testing, indicating a problem in the software.

- **DevOps:** A set of practices that combines development (Dev) and IT operations (Ops) to shorten the software development lifecycle and improve collaboration and deployment processes.

- **Exploratory Testing:** A testing approach where testers explore the software, learn about its functionality, and identify defects without predefined test cases.

- **Functional Testing:** Testing that focuses on the functional aspects of software to ensure that it performs its intended tasks correctly.

- **Growth Mindset:** A belief that intelligence and abilities can be developed through dedication and effort, leading to a willingness to learn and embrace challenges.

- **Regression Testing:** Testing conducted to ensure that new code changes do not adversely affect existing functionality.

- **Risk Management:** The process of identifying, assessing, prioritising, and mitigating risks that may affect the quality or success of a project.

- **Sprint:** A time-boxed iteration in Agile development, typically lasting two to four weeks, during which specific work is completed.

- **Test Case:** A detailed set of instructions or conditions that specify how a particular aspect of software should be tested.

- **Test Coverage:** A measure of how much of a software application has been tested, often expressed as a percentage.

- **Test Driven Development (TDD):** A development approach where tests are written before writing the code, guiding the development process.

- **User Acceptance Testing (UAT):** A type of testing where end-users or stakeholders validate that the software meets their requirements and expectations.

- **Usability Testing:** Testing conducted to evaluate how user-friendly a software application is by observing real users interacting with it.

- **Waterfall Model:** A traditional linear software development model where each phase must be completed before the next one begins.

Appendix B: Recommended Resources for QA Professionals

In the dynamic field of Quality Assurance (QA), continuous learning and staying informed about industry trends, tools, and best practices are essential. This appendix provides a list of recommended resources that can help QA professionals expand their knowledge and expertise.

1. Books

- "Foundations of Software Testing ISTQB Certification" by Rex Black (Author), Erik van Veenendaal (Author), Dorothy Graham (Author)

- "Testing Computer Software" by Cem Kaner, Jack Falk, and Hung Q. Nguyen

- "Agile Testing: A Practical Guide for Testers and Agile Teams" by Lisa Crispin and Janet Gregory

- "Continuous Delivery: Reliable Software Releases through Build, Test, and Deployment Automation" by Jez Humble and David Farley

- "Explore It!: Reduce Risk and Increase Confidence with Exploratory Testing" by Elisabeth Hendrickson

- "Buddha in Testing : Finding Peace in Chaos" by Pradeep Soundararajan

2. Websites and Blogs

- <u>QAXcellence</u>: One stop solution for modern day testing.

- <u>Ministry of Testing</u>: Offers a wealth of articles, webinars, and resources for software testers.

- <u>Software Testing Help</u>: Provides tutorials, articles, and tools for software testing professionals.

- <u>Test Automation University</u>: Offers free courses on various automation testing tools and practices.

- <u>TestProject Blog</u>: Covers topics related to test automation, best practices, and industry trends.

3. Forums and Communities

- <u>Stack Overflow - Testing</u>: A community where you can ask and answer questions related to software testing.

- <u>Reddit - Software Testing</u>: A subreddit for discussions on software testing and QA.

- <u>LinkedIn Groups</u>: Join relevant LinkedIn groups such as "Software Testing and Quality Assurance," "QA &

Testing Jobs Worldwide," and others to connect with professionals in the field.

4. Online Courses and Training

- <u>Coursera</u>: Offers courses on software testing, Agile, and related topics from universities and institutions.

- <u>MoolyaEd</u>: It's a Software Testing Training institute, which aims to build industry ready Software Testers

- <u>Udemy</u>: Provides a wide range of QA and testing courses, including automation and performance testing.

5. Professional Organizations

- <u>ISTQB - International Software Testing Qualifications Board</u>: Offers certification and resources for software testers.

- <u>ASTQB - American Software Testing Qualifications Board</u>: Provides software testing certification programs.

6. QA and Testing Tools

- <u>Selenium</u>: An open-source tool for browser automation.

- <u>Playright</u>: Playwright enables reliable end-to-end testing for modern web apps. · Any browser Any platform One API · Resilient No flaky tests · No trade-offs No limits.

- <u>Jenkins</u>: An open-source automation server for building, testing, and deploying software.

- <u>JIRA</u>: A popular issue and project tracking tool often used in Agile development.

7. Podcasts

- <u>Test Talks</u>: Features interviews and discussions with software testing professionals.

- <u>The Testing Show</u>: Covers various aspects of software testing and quality assurance.

8. YouTube Channels

- <u>Tricentis</u>: Provides videos on software testing, test automation, and best practices.

- <u>Test Automation University</u>: Offers video tutorials on test automation tools and practices.

- <u>Pavan Kumar</u>: Offers educational videos on software testing & automation tools.

- <u>Rahul Shetty</u>: Provides live and offline videos on software testing & test automation.

- <u>Naveen Automation Lab</u>: Offers test automation training, courses and consultation

9. Social Media

- Follow influential QA professionals, organisations, and hashtags related to software testing on platforms like Twitter and LinkedIn to stay updated with the latest news and discussions.

These resources can serve as valuable references and tools for QA professionals as they continue their journey towards QA excellence.

Are you ready to embark on a journey towards QA excellence?

In this comprehensive guide, you've explored the essential principles and practices that define the world of Quality Assurance (QA). From mastering the art of effective test case design to harnessing the power of test automation, from managing risks strategically to leveraging the insights provided by metrics and reporting, this book has been your trusted companion on the path to QA excellence.

But QA excellence is not a destination; it's a continuous quest, and your journey is far from over. In the dynamic landscapes of Agile, DevOps, AI, and Machine Learning, QA professionals must adapt, innovate, and embrace change like never before. This book has equipped you with the knowledge, mindset, and skills needed to thrive in these evolving environments.

As you close this book, remember that your pursuit of QA excellence is not just about achieving perfection but about the commitment to continuous learning, improvement, and ethical practice. It's about fostering effective collaboration, communicating with clarity, and maintaining resilience in the face of challenges.

Thank you for joining me on this journey. Your dedication to QA excellence will not only shape the quality of software and products but also contribute to the ever-evolving field of Quality Assurance itself.

Now, armed with the knowledge and principles shared in these pages, go forth and continue your quest for Quality Assurance excellence. Your journey has just begun.

Happy Testing....
Shree Narayan Jha